WORLD MYTHS AND LEGENDS II

D0668904

Central America

Martha Schmitt

Fearon/Janus/Quercus
Belmont, CA

Simon & Schuster Education Group

World Myths and Legends
Greek and Roman
Ancient Middle Eastern
Norse
African
Far Eastern
Celtic
Native American
Regional American

World Myths and Legends II
India
Russia
Europe
South America
The Caribbean
Central America
Mexico
Southeast Asia

Series Editor: Joseph T. Curran
Cover Designer: Dianne Platner
Text Designer: Teresa A. Holden
Interior Illustrations: Mary Beth Gaitskill
Cover Photo: The Granger Collection, New York

Library of Congress Catalog Card Number: 92–72302
ISBN 0–8224–4633–2
Printed in the United States of America
2. 10 9 8 7 6 5 4 3 2
EB

CONTENTS

3 Lessons Learned

4 Animal Tales

An Introduction to the Myths and Legends of Central America

Central America consists of the countries of Guatemala, Belize, El Salvador, Honduras, Nicaragua, Costa Rica, and Panama. These countries occupy a bridge of land that connects North and South America. This area has been home to many groups of native people, who have passed on their myths and legends both orally and in writing.

The largest group of native people in Central America are the Maya. Between A.D. 250 and A.D. 900, the Maya developed a magnificient civilization. In Guatemala and Mexico, they built great cities with palaces and pyramids. The Maya also invented an advanced system of writing. Their empire extended beyond Mexico and Guatemala into Belize, Honduras, and El Salvador.

Today, there are about 5 million Maya. They belong to a number of tribes and speak a number of languages. However, all the languages are related because they all come from the ancient Mayan language. In Guatemala, these branches include the Cakchiquel, Chorti, Ixil, Kanhobal, Kekchi,

Mopan, Mam, Quiche, and Tzutuhil. The Chorti, Mopan, and Kekchi extend into Honduras and Belize.

The Guatemalan Maya make up the largest native culture in Central America, and so their stories are most numerous in this book. They have told their stories at home, during their work breaks, around campfires, and at funerals. Storytelling has been a way to pass on beliefs and customs.

The main source of Guatemalan Mayan myths is the *Popol Vuh*, or Council Book, written in the 1500s. The story "The Deadly Game" is based on a central myth in the *Popol Vuh*.

Other native groups in Central America include the Jicaque of Honduras, the Pipil of El Salvador, the Mískito of Nicaragua, the Cabécar of Costa Rica, and the Cuna of Panama. To varying degrees, all of these groups have also preserved their tradition of oral storytelling. This book provides a sampling of those stories.

These myths and legends include a cast of unusual characters—gods, spirits, giants, witches, kings, plant people, and talking animals. They represent the rich tradition of storytelling in Central America.

In the Beginning

This story about the creation of the world comes from the Cuna of Panama. In it, the god Olocupinele makes the earth and the first people.

Olocupinele made the whole world. He created the earth, the sun, the moon, and the stars. He made the ocean and the wind. He made everything out of some of his own spirit, wisdom, and love.

Olocupinele prepared the earth for his children, the Cunas. He made it soft, gentle, and warm. He formed the mountains and set them between two oceans. In the mountains, he made green valleys, where he planted shade trees. Olocupinele prepared wonderful gardens with corn and melons. He caused the rain to fall and the rivers to flow. He made the fish, birds, and other animals on the earth.

Olocupinele wanted to do everything he could for the Cunas. So he made gems, spices, clay, and dyes. He even created the rainbow with its many colors so that the Cunas could enjoy its beauty.

The earth Olocupinele made

When Olocupinele finished, the earth was full of life. It was the first spring. Then Olocupinele created the first Cuna men and women. He made them like himself. They were tall and proud, like gods, and they had golden skin and black, straight hair.

To each person, Olocupinele gave a soul and a special gift. Some people received skill in hunting and others in fishing. Some people were good at farming and others at making music.

One at a time, Olocupinele set each person gently on earth. He put the people in a beautiful garden. The people did not know what to do or how to live, though. They felt blinded by the sunlight, and they huddled together in the shade.

So Olocupinele created a special person, also made from his spirit, wisdom, and love. This person was Piler, the first leader of the Cunas.

Piler was born with special knowledge. He said to the other people, "Don't be afraid! Come out into the light! Each of us is different and beautiful. We are all brothers and sisters."

Smiling, Piler went on, "We must love the earth, our mother. As we get our food and drink from her, we must respect and take care of her."

Then Piler put one hand on a rock and another on a flower. He continued, "We are Olocupinele's children, caretakers of the earth. As the rock does not hurt the flower, so we must not harm one another. Just as we cannot create life, so we must not take away life. We must take care of all that lives. Our father, Olocupinele, so wishes."

In this way, the Cunas were taught to love Olocupinele, the earth, themselves, and one another.

1. *How did the people act when they were first put on earth?*
2. *How was Piler different from the other people?*
3. *According to Piler, how should people treat the earth?*

The Sun Dancer

This myth comes from the Maya of Guatemala. It gives an unusual explanation of where the sun came from.

One day long ago, a man was walking through the forest. It was a hot afternoon, and the man became tired. Wanting to take a nap, the man looked for a safe spot. He chose a large tree with wide branches.

The man climbed up the tree and nestled in the branches. Within a short time, he fell asleep. The man was so tired that he slept into the evening.

During the evening, three thieves were passing through the forest. They carried a large trunk, in which they kept all their stolen goods.

It so happened that the thieves decided to camp under the tree in which the man was sleeping. They did not notice the man high above them.

The thieves made a campfire, over which they roasted some meat. After they ate, the three men lay down and went to sleep.

During the night, the man who was in the

tree awoke. He smelled the campfire below. Looking down, he could see the three sleeping men. Quietly, he climbed down the tree and looked around.

The man crept up to the fire, around which some leftover meat was lying. Since the man was hungry, he ate his fill of the food. He took care to be very quiet and not wake the thieves.

As he was finishing eating, the man noticed the large trunk lying near the sleeping men. He wondered what the men might be carrying in the trunk. Carefully and quietly, the man sneaked up to the trunk and opened it.

Inside the trunk lay beautiful clothes of bright colors. The clothes were made of soft cotton, and they were finely embroidered.

One by one, the man then took out each garment and tried it on. He enjoyed the feel of the soft cloth and the beauty of the embroidery.

The last garment in the chest was a brilliant red cape. As he put on the cape, the man felt very special. He had never worn such a fine cape! Then a strange feeling passed through his body. He felt as if something was taking over his body.

Suddenly, the man's legs started to move, and without warning his body began to dance. The man could not stop the movement. His body whirled around, leapt into the air, and landed gracefully on the ground again. The man danced wildly. The brilliant red cape whirled around him. His body moved faster and faster.

The noise of the dancing awoke one of the thieves, who slowly opened his eyes. He blinked, thinking, "This must be a dream! Surely, there isn't really a man dressed in red dancing around the fire!"

As the thief came to his senses, he realized that he was not dreaming. The thief thought, "There really is a man dressed in bright red! There is a madman dancing around the fire!"

"Ahhhh!" the thief screamed. The scream awoke his two friends, who then saw the man in red, too.

"Oh, no!" screamed another of the thieves. "It's an evil spirit. It's come to eat us! We must get away from here."

Immediately, all the thieves jumped up in fright. They ran far into the forest as fast as they could.

The man in the red cape paid no attention

to the thieves. He just kept on dancing with abandon. He began shouting loudly with joy. His legs carried him away from the fire and through the forest. Around the trees he glided, dancing more and more wildly with each step.

Soon the man came to the edge of a steep cliff. The cliff was so steep that it seemed like the edge of the earth. The dancing man paid no attention and did not stop at the cliff's edge, however. Without a pause, he stepped over the edge and into the air.

The man felt light and free in the air. Instead of falling, though, he continued dancing through the air with his red cape swirling around him. His body rose higher and higher.

Soon the man was so high that he looked like a great red ball in the sky. A bright, warm light began to flow from him.

The dancing man in the brilliant red cape became the sun.

1. *What happened when the man tried on the red cape?*
2. *What did the thieves think the dancing man was?*
3. *How did the dancing man become the sun?*

Sun Finds a Wife

This story comes from the Maya of Guatemala. Some of the Maya used to regard the moon as the sun's wife. This story tells how the sun met and married his wife, who became the moon. At the beginning of the tale, the sun lives on the earth as a man, and the moon does not yet exist.

Sun Sees the King's Daughter

Long ago, there was a king who had magic powers. This king had a beautiful daughter whom he loved dearly. He was a strict father, however, and he expected his daughter to obey him.

One day, Sun saw the beautiful daughter outside in the king's garden. He immediately wanted her to be his wife. So he thought about how he might impress her.

Sun decided to pose as a great hunter. He would make the woman think that he could kill game every day, which was difficult to do. Then the woman would think that Sun would be a good provider and so would make a good husband.

The next day, Sun shot a deer in the woods and slung it over his shoulder. Then he walked along the path past the woman's house. The woman could see Sun carrying the deer.

That night, Sun cut the skin off the deer and stuffed the skin with ashes. He hid the stuffed deerskin in the woods where he could get it when he needed it. He planned to make the woman think that he could get a deer every day.

The next morning, Sun went to the woods for the stuffed deerskin. He slung it over his shoulder and walked past the woman's house. The woman noticed this hunter carrying what she thought was another deer.

Sun carried the deerskin past the woman's house the next day and again the next. Every time the woman saw Sun, she thought he had killed another deer.

One day, the woman washed some corn in a bowl of water. She threw out the water on the path near her house.

Later that day, Sun came along the path with his stuffed deerskin. He slipped on the water, and he dropped the deerskin. The deerskin hit the ground and burst open, causing all the ashes to fall out.

Sun with his stuffed deerskin

The woman saw what happened. She knew then that the man had not killed many deer after all. He had been carrying the same deer past her house every day.

Sun felt rather foolish. To avoid having to explain his actions, he turned himself into a hummingbird. He flew among the flowers in the king's garden. He could still see the king's daughter. She, however, did not know he was Sun.

The Flight

The woman saw the pretty hummingbird and wanted it as a pet.

"Father, come here," the daughter called. "See that hummingbird? I would like to have him. Can you shoot him with your magic blowgun?"

To please his daughter, the king shot the bird. He gave the stunned little bird to his daughter. The daughter was happy to have the bird, and she kept it with her all day. She took it with her into her room that night.

During the night, the hummingbird woke up. He changed back into a man at once. He wanted to tell the woman who he was and persuade her to go away with him.

"Wake up," Sun said to the woman. "Come

with me. Let's go away from here."

The woman woke up and recognized the man who had carried the deer. She laughed when he told her all he had done to impress her. She wanted to go with Sun, but she was afraid to run away.

"My father has ordered me never to leave here without him," she told Sun. "He has a magic stone that he can look into. The stone will show him where we have gone. He also has a magic blowgun that he could use to kill us. He would be very angry at me for leaving."

"I, too, have some magic powers," Sun said. "I will fix the stone and the blowgun."

Sun quickly found the stone. In a great hurry, he rubbed it with dye. Next he found the blowgun and put chili pepper inside it.

Then Sun and the woman ran away together.

The next morning, when the king awoke, he could not find his daughter. He took his magic stone and tried to look into it. At first, he could not see through the dye. Then he found a spot that Sun had missed in his rush to leave. Looking through this spot, the king saw his daughter and Sun crossing a river in a canoe.

Quickly, the king grabbed his magic blowgun and started to suck in his breath before blowing. In with his breath came the hot chili pepper. The chili pepper got in his mouth and made him cough violently. His mouth burned, and his eyes ran.

The King's Revenge

Now the king was very angry. He called on a lightning bolt to strike his daughter and the man. The lightning set out to obey the king's command.

Sun, however, saw the lightning coming.

"Your father is trying to kill us," he yelled to the woman. "Dive into the water!"

Sun and the king's daughter both jumped into the water. Sun turned himself into a turtle and the woman into a crab. They both swam toward the bottom of the river.

The king's daughter did not swim fast enough, however. The lightning bolt hit her and killed her. The woman's blood flowed out over the water.

Sun swam far down, so the lightning bolt did not reach him. When he came back up, he saw the woman's blood everywhere. He was heartbroken and tried to think of a way to regain the woman he wanted to marry.

Sun and the Woman Marry

Sun looked around in the river. He saw dragonflies flying on top of the water. Sun called all the dragonflies together and said, "Please gather up this blood for me."

The dragonflies collected the blood in bottles and gave them to Sun. Then Sun went ashore with the bottles. He found a safe place to leave the bottles for a time.

After three weeks, Sun returned for the bottles and opened each one. Out of the first bottle came snakes. Out of the next came wasps. He opened more bottles, and more creatures came out. Then he came to the last bottle. Out of it came the king's daughter, but she was very small.

Sun knew how to make the woman larger again. He took the king's daughter with him and looked for a deer in the woods. When he found a deer, Sun told him to step over the woman three times. The deer obeyed, and the woman became her full size again. She greeted Sun happily and agreed that they should marry.

Sun wanted to go into the sky, away from the king and all the troubles on earth. The daughter agreed that they should both go into the sky.

"I can be the light of the day, and you can be the light of the night," Sun said.

So, the king's daughter married Sun, and she became Moon.

1. *What did Sun carry past the woman's house the second day?*
2. *How could the king see through the magic stone covered with dye?*
3. *Who collected the woman's blood for Sun?*

How the Sea Was Made

The Cabécar of Costa Rica tell this story about how the sea was formed. In this myth, the god who creates the world is named Sibú.

Long ago, there was no earth. There was just a big rock in place of the earth. There was nowhere for people to live.

Sibú looked down from his house in the sky. He said, "I want to make a home for people. That rock would not make a good home. I must make the earth."

Sibú called to Sea, who was then a beautiful woman with long, lovely hair. He told her, "Go to visit Thunder. Tell him to come to me. I want to talk with him about making the earth."

Sea did as Sibú asked, but Thunder would not come. So Sea returned to Sibú and told him what had happened.

Sibú thought Sea could change Thunder's mind if she were to take Sibú's hiking stick to Thunder. He said, "Tell Thunder he can use my staff for his trip here. He can lean on it when he gets tired."

Sea going to visit Thunder

Again, Sea did as Sibú asked. However, Thunder would not take the staff.

Thunder said to Sea, "I do not want to visit Sibú. I do not want his staff, but you should use it for your trip back to Sibú. Remember this, however! Take good care of the staff. Never put it down."

Sea did not think Thunder's words were important. "How silly to think I can't put this stick down! What harm could come from it?" she thought.

So on the trip back, Sea put down the staff and lost it. She looked and looked, but she couldn't find the staff anywhere.

As Sea was searching for the staff, she came across a poisonous snake. The snake was startled, and it bit Sea, killing her instantly.

When Sibú saw that Sea was dead, he came for her and prepared her for burial. Just as he was doing so, though, strange things began to happen to Sea's body. First, her body began to swell. Then, it became a tree and rose up into the air. Sea's hair became leaves, and birds came to make their nests there.

The tree kept on growing and growing. Finally, it grew so tall that it broke through the sky, which was Sibú's house. Sibú did not like having this tree sticking into his house. He called two birds.

"Grab the top of the tree and bend it until it makes a circle," Sibú directed the birds.

When the birds carried out Sibú's order, the tree fell down from the sky. It then changed into water. There was so much water that it formed the sea. Some parts of the tree turned into the creatures of the sea. The bird nests became turtles, and the leaves of the tree changed into crabs. The surf began to pound.

Sibú was glad to have the tree out of his sky. He also had a beginning for the earth, where people could live. The sea was that beginning.

Now there is still the sea, and there are still turtles and crabs in the sea. We know, too, that the sound of the surf is an echo. It echoes the wind that blew through the leaves of the tree, which was once Sea's body.

1. *Why did Sibú send his staff to Thunder?*
2. *What happened to Sea's dead body?*
3. *What happened to the tree after the birds bent it into a circle?*

The Rumbling Volcano

Guatemala is a country with many volcanoes, some of them active. At times, there are earthquakes. The Mayas tell this story that explains the rumbling of one volcano and the cause of earthquakes. The story centers around a giant named Sipac, who appears in many Mayan myths.

Once there was a strong giant named Sipac. He could swim a river without taking a breath, and he could pick up volcanoes in his hands. This giant was always hungry. He would do anything to get food.

To get bread, Sipac found some people who were willing to trade with him. Since they wanted the volcanoes, they would give Sipac large loaves of bread in exchange for the volcanoes. So Sipac began collecting volcanoes.

One day, Sipac was picking up a volcano not far from a river. He happened to see three women with long hair bathing in the river. The women were the three corn spirits, who watched over the cornfields. They had the power to make the harvests good or poor.

Sipac

Sipac did not know who the women were, however. He only noticed how beautiful they were. He immediately fell in love with the three women. Sipac walked over to the river and put down the volcano he was carrying at the time.

"Hello," said Sipac to the women. "You are all so beautiful that I would like to marry you. Will you be my wives? I'll take good care of you because I'm big and strong. I can sell volcanoes to buy you good food and fine clothes. I'll make sure you always have whatever you want."

"Well," the corn spirits answered, "maybe we can make a deal. We like to eat food that comes from the river. We eat fish and frogs and crabs. If you catch all our food in the river, we'll marry you."

"All right," said Sipac, happy that the women had agreed. He thought it would be easy to get the food the women wanted.

The three corn spirits did not really plan to marry Sipac, however.

One of the women pointed to a place deep in the river. She said, "Sipac, I'm hungry right now. There is a rock on the bottom of the river. If you dive down and look, there may be a crab under it. Will you please go there and get a crab for me?"

"Oh, yes," answered Sipac. "I'd be happy to do that. I'll have a crab for you in just one minute!"

The giant took a deep breath and dived into the water. On the bottom, he found the rock the woman had spoken about. He started looking around and under it. He searched for many minutes, but he couldn't find a crab.

"What's taking so long?" the woman called to Sipac after a while.

"I can't find a crab," answered the giant from under the water.

"Then come back up. I'll show you another spot to look," said the woman.

Sipac came up out of the river, wet and out of breath. He was embarrassed that he had not found a crab. He realized that the work might not be as easy as he had thought.

"There's a big rock way over there," the woman said. "I know there's a crab under it. We always find crabs there. However, you'll have to crawl under the rock. Maybe we should tie a chain around you. Then if you get stuck, we can pull you out."

Sipac was determined to find a crab this time. So he agreed to the woman's idea. He let the women tie a chain around his hands and feet. Then he dived deep into the water again. He found the rock and started to crawl under it.

After Sipac was all the way under the rock, the three women dived in the river. They swam to the rock, and they all pushed hard on it. They pushed it down as far as they could. Sipac was still under the rock, with his hands and feet in chains.

Sipac shook his chains and rolled around trying to get loose, but he was stuck. He realized that the three beautiful women had tricked him.

The three corn spirits left Sipac under the rock, where he remains today. The volcano that he put down near the river is now called Sipac.

Sometimes, the earth rumbles near this volcano. The noise comes from Sipac shaking his chains. At times, the earth moves with great force in many places. This earthquake is caused by Sipac turning over, still trying to get loose from his chains.

1. *Why was Sipac collecting volcanoes?*
2. *Why did Sipac dive into the water and crawl under the big rock?*
3. *According to this myth, what is the cause of earthquakes?*

The Music Maker

The Maya of Guatemala play a musical instrument called a chirimía. The chirimía is a woodwind instrument somewhat like an oboe. The Spanish introduced the chirimía to the Maya. This myth, however, tells a different story about how the Maya learned about the chirimía.

The Unhappy Daughter

Long ago, there lived a Maya king and his beautiful daughter, Nima-cux. The king loved his daughter, and the daughter loved her father. The two spent much time together, and they were close friends.

For many years, Nima-cux was a cheerful young woman. In time, however, Nima-cux began to change. She became moody and would not talk to her father. She never smiled anymore, and she asked to be left alone.

The king did not understand what was wrong with his daughter. He tried everything he could think of to make her happy again.

First, the king brought his daughter some colorful birds as pets. Nima-cux took no interest at all in the birds.

Then the king gave Nima-cux beautiful beads. She just tossed the beads aside as if they were nothing.

Next, the king brought musicians to the palace to sing for his daughter. Nima-cux listened in silence, never smiling.

Then the king invited some young people to the palace to play games with Nima-cux. Again, she took no interest.

Not knowing what else to do, the king called together some wise men.

"You must help me," the king told them. "I don't know what to do for my daughter. She is unhappy and takes no interest in anything. She stays in her room most of the time and talks to no one."

The wise men asked the king to leave them alone for a while. Then they talked among themselves and came up with an idea for the king.

"We do have an idea for helping your daughter," the wise men told the king. "You know, your daughter is now of the age to be married. You should see if she takes an interest in marrying."

"I will do that," said the king.

The Suitors

So the king issued an order throughout his land. He sent messengers to all the young noblemen. He set a day that the men should come to the palace. Then the king would allow the princess to choose a husband from among the young noblemen.

On the appointed day, all the young noblemen came to the palace. The men were dressed in their finest clothes and wore gold and feathers.

Each young nobleman presented himself to the king and his daughter. Each one told what his special talent was. Some of the men were very strong, others were great hunters, and still others had much gold. The princess was not impressed with any of the men, however.

Finally as the day was almost ending, a young man walked up the path to the palace. Although he was a nobleman, he was not particularly well-dressed. He wore no gold or feathers. As the man walked, he sang a beautiful song. His voice was rich and full.

The princess smiled when she heard the man's voice. Her eyes lit up, and she took obvious pleasure in the man's singing.

The king was overjoyed to see the change

in his daughter. He immediately called the young man.

"Come here, young man," the king said. "I see that your singing pleases my daughter. You shall be the one to marry the princess."

Before the young man could answer, the princess spoke.

Smiling, Nima-cux said, "Your singing does please me. I have never heard any man sing more beautifully. The birds have lovelier songs, though. When you can sing like a bird, I will marry you."

"I will happily do anything for you," the nobleman answered. "I will try to learn to sing like a bird. You must give me some time to study the birds' songs, however, and to practice."

So the king and princess agreed that the man should have time to practice. Then they set a day when he should come back to the palace and sing for them.

The Spirit of the Forest

The young man left the palace and went to stay in the forest. There, he listened to the birds' singing. He tried to match their songs. For many days, he listened and practiced.

Even though he practiced every day,

however, the young man could not sing like the birds. The day for him to return to the palace was drawing near. Sitting on a log in the woods, the man grew sad.

"I guess I will have to give up," the man said to himself. "It's no use. There's just no way I can sing as beautifully as one of these birds."

Suddenly, the Spirit of the Forest appeared to the man. The Spirit smiled and seemed friendly, and so the young man was not afraid.

"What's wrong?" the Spirit asked the young man.

The man answered, "I want to marry the king's daughter, but she will marry me only on one condition. It is that I must be able to sing like a bird. I've tried and tried for many days, but I cannot match the singing of the birds. So it appears that I will not be able to marry the princess."

"I can help you," said the Spirit. "Do as I tell you. Take your knife and cut a branch from one of the trees. Then bring the branch to me."

The young man chose a tree and cut a sturdy branch from it. Then he brought the branch to the Spirit.

Using the man's knife, the Spirit of the Forest scraped out the center of the branch and made a tube. Then the Spirit cut holes in the tube.

"Watch how I play this and then do the same thing," said the Spirit. "I have made you a chirimía. Its music is as beautiful as a bird singing."

The young man watched closely as the Spirit played the instrument. Then the man took the instrument, blew into it, and moved his fingers along the holes.

The Spirit told the man, "Practice playing the chirimía until you can make beautiful music. Then go and play for the princess. She will love your music, and she will be happy to marry you."

Then the Spirit disappeared.

The young man spent the next few days playing the chirimía. At last, he was satisfied with his playing. The music he made sounded as beautiful as a singing bird.

The young man returned to the palace and asked for the king and his daughter. He played the chirimía for them. Nima-cux and her father listened in wonder. This was the most beautiful music they had ever heard!

"I would be happy to marry you now," the

princess told the young man. From that day on, Nima-cux was happy again. The king rejoiced, and soon Nima-cux and the young man were married.

In this way, the Maya learned about the chirimía.

1. *Why did the king call the wise men together?*
2. *On what condition did the princess agree to marry the young man?*
3. *How did the young man learn to play the chirimía?*

The Grapefruit Wife

This story from the Maya of Guatemala is about a prince who has an unusual idea. He decides he wants a wife from the world of plants.

The Old Man's Gifts

Long ago, a king had a son who wanted to marry. However, the son did not want an ordinary wife.

"Father," the son said, "I want a wife who comes from the world of plants."

The king thought his son's idea was a little odd. However, the king did not try to stop his son.

One day, the prince went for a long walk in the forest, looking at the plants. Along the forest path, he met an old man.

"What are you doing?" asked the old man.

"I'm looking for a wife from among the plants," answered the prince.

"You will find her, but you will have many difficulties," the old man said. "Take this stone, this thorn, and this cup with water. You will need them."

So the prince took the stone, thorn, and

cup and continued on his way. After a short
time, he saw a tree with ripe grapefruits.
Since he was thirsty, the prince picked one of
the grapefruits to drink its juice.

Cutting the fruit open, he whispered,
"Juice, please."

The grapefruit was dry inside, however.
The prince cut another grapefruit, but it was
the same. He picked a third grapefruit and
whispered the same words. Suddenly, the
fruit turned into a beautiful woman who
stood smiling at him. The prince was
amazed.

"You're just what I've been dreaming of,"
said the prince. "Do come with me."

The woman took the prince's hand, and
they started back to his father's house.
Within a short time, however, the prince and
the woman heard footsteps close behind
them. They realized they were being followed
by robbers.

The prince remembered the old man's
words and the three things the old man had
given him. The prince threw down the thorn
in front of the robbers. Immediately, a great
thorn bush grew up to block the robbers'
path. The prince and the woman then
hurried on.

The prince picking a grapefruit

After a short time, the couple again heard footsteps behind them. The robbers had cut through the thorn bush. This time, the prince threw the stone down onto the path behind him. At once, a large hill arose in front of the robbers. Again, the prince and the grapefruit woman continued on their way. After a short time, they heard the robbers behind them once more. The robbers had climbed over the hill.

"This is the last of the old man's gifts," said the prince. "I hope this works." He threw down the cup of water on the path where they had just been.

Suddenly, an ocean spread out behind the prince and the woman. This time the robbers were stopped because they drowned in the water. Feeling safe at last, the prince and the grapefruit woman continued on their way.

A New Problem

After walking for some time, the grapefruit woman spotted a stream near the path. She left the prince to get a drink from the stream. As she leaned over the water, the grapefruit woman saw the reflection of another face. It was the face of an ugly witch who had come up behind her.

"Ah, how beautiful I am!" said the witch, looking at her reflection in the stream.

"You may think you're beautiful, but you really are ugly," said the grapefruit woman.

The witch did not want to hear this. She thought her burned, wrinkled skin really was beautiful. In anger, she stuck the grapefruit woman with a thorn. The witch's thorn made the grapefruit woman turn into a dove, which flew away.

Just then, the prince came to see what was taking so long. The witch clouded the prince's eyes so that he did not see her exactly as she was.

"You look a little bit different," said the prince. "Are you really the same grapefruit woman?"

"Oh, yes, I am," answered the witch. "I'm just getting a little sunburned out here. That is all."

The prince and the witch walked together the rest of the way to the king's house. The prince took the witch proudly to his father to introduce her.

"This is the woman I've chosen to marry, Father. She came from a grapefruit," the prince said to the king.

The king was surprised when he saw the

woman. He said quietly to his son, "She's rather ugly, but perhaps you do not care."

"Oh, she's just a little sunburned from the long walk," answered the prince.

Just at that time a dove flew into the king's garden, calling, "Prince, prince." The gardener came to tell the prince.

"Catch the dove for me," the prince ordered the gardener.

So the gardener caught the dove, put it in a cage, and gave it to the prince. The prince decided to keep the dove as a pet.

The Witch and the Dove

Before the prince could marry the witch, a war broke out in the king's land. Since his father was old, the prince left to lead the army in his father's place.

While the prince was gone, the witch decided to get rid of the dove. She killed the dove and asked the cook to fix it for dinner.

As the cook was cutting up the dove, its heart called out, "Don't cook me! Plant me in the garden." The cook was shocked and afraid. He immediately ran out to the garden and planted the heart.

After a short time, a grapefruit tree grew up where the dove's heart was planted. The tree was ripe with fruit when the prince returned from the war.

Before the day the prince would marry the witch, there was a celebration for the king's birthday. The prince went to the tree to pick a grapefruit for his father. As he took a grapefruit, he remembered the day he first found his grapefruit woman.

"Juice, please," he whispered gently to the grapefruit.

Suddenly, the beautiful grapefruit woman stood before him. The prince realized the witch had fooled him. He ran to find the witch, but she was gone.

The prince was very happy to be rid of the witch. He was even more happy to have found the grapefruit woman once again. The grapefruit woman was just as pleased to rejoin the prince.

The prince and the grapefruit woman wasted no time, and they were soon married. Neither of them ever saw the witch again. They lived happily together for all the rest of their lives.

1. *What three things did the old man give the prince?*
2. *How did the prince lose the grapefruit woman?*
3. *How did the prince find the grapefruit woman again?*

The Bird Man

In this story from the Maya of Guatemala, a man enters the world of birds. He becomes a vulture, which is commonly called a buzzard. This bird eats the remains of dead animals.

Long ago, there was a man who made his living by farming. Every day, the man would go out to work in his field. He had to clear the field of trees and brush to prepare it for planting corn.

This work was very hard, and the man did not like it.

The man grew very lazy. Instead of working in his field, he would lie down and rest most of the day.

One day, the man went out to his field as usual. He sat down to rest and leaned back against a large stone. Gazing up at the sky, he saw a buzzard flying overhead.

"What a great life that buzzard has!" the man thought to himself. "He just flies around as he pleases. He doesn't have to work at all for his food."

"Come down here!" the man called to the buzzard.

The buzzard flew down and landed on the ground next to the man.

"What do you want?" asked the buzzard.

"How would you like to change places with me?" the man asked. "I would like to have your life, just flying around all day. Then I'd never have to work in the field. I'm sick of this work."

"Well," said the buzzard, "you'd have to eat dead, rotting meat. That's what buzzards eat—dead animals."

"I know I could do that," said the man. "It wouldn't bother me at all. At least I wouldn't have to hunt and kill the animals to have meat."

"All right, then," said the buzzard. "Let's change places."

To make the change, the buzzard and the man then jumped up in the air together three times. The man turned into a buzzard, and the buzzard turned into a man.

The man who was now a buzzard flew into the sky. He soared over the trees and the fields and the hills. He felt free and happy.

"This life of a bird is just right for me!" the man thought.

Meanwhile, the buzzard who was now a man started working in the field. He cleared away the brush for several hours. He grew hot and sweaty and hungry. At lunchtime, the buzzard man went home to eat.

When the buzzard man walked in the door, the wife said, "Oh, my! You smell awful! What's wrong with you?"

"Nothing's wrong with me," answered the buzzard man. "I've just been working in the field all morning. I smell from sweating. Clearing the field is hard work, and the sun is hot."

Meanwhile, the woman's real husband had also gotten hungry. He didn't want to look for a dead animal to eat, however. Now that he was hungry, the thought of dead, rotting meat made him sick. He decided that he had already had enough of being a bird. He wanted to change back into a man and go back home to eat.

So he flew to the ground and jumped up into the air three times. Nothing happened. He couldn't change back into a man. He realized he would always be a buzzard.

"What will I do?" thought the man who was now a buzzard. "I want to go home to eat good food."

So he flew to his house and went in through the open door.

The man's wife screamed, "Why did that buzzard fly into our house? This is awful! I have to get that bird out of here."

The woman got a big stick and started chasing and hitting the bird. The buzzard would not leave the house, however.

"Stop that!" yelled the buzzard man. "That's your husband you're hitting. I am the one who is really a buzzard. That's why I smell so bad. Your husband wanted to change places with me. He wanted to be a buzzard so that he wouldn't have to work anymore. So I became a man, and he became a buzzard."

"Well, change back right now!" the woman yelled. "Change places again, and then get out of here."

"No, I'm sorry," the buzzard who was now a man replied. "Now we can never change back. I have to remain a man, and he has to remain a buzzard."

The woman sat down and began to cry. She wanted her own husband back, even though he was lazy. The change was forever, however, and there was nothing anyone could do.

The unwelcome buzzard

1. *Why did the man want to become a buzzard?*
2. *How did the man feel about being a buzzard?*
3. *What happened when the man tried to change from a buzzard into a man again?*

How the World Was Saved

This story comes from the Jicaque of Honduras. It tells about a man's trip to the underworld, the land of the dead. According to Jicaque myths, the underworld lies below the earth. In the myths, the underworld has a number of large posts that hold up the earth.

Long ago, three thieves died and went to the underworld. These thieves, who were bad men on earth, immediately began to cause trouble in the underworld. They started to dig up the posts that held up the earth.

At this time, a man on earth was in the forest, hunting deer with a bow and arrows. He was an unusually strong man.

A god appeared to this hunter. "You must go to the underworld," the god said. "Three men are trying to destroy the earth. They are digging up the posts. If they succeed, the earth will fall over. You must stop them."

"How can I go to the underworld?" asked the hunter.

"I will help," the god said. "I will use my power to send you to the underworld. You use your strength to stop the evil men."

Digging up the posts

"I will go and do what I can," said the hunter.

So the hunter went to the underworld as the god had asked. He found the three men hard at work, digging up the posts. One post was already loose. The earth was in great danger.

"Stop that!" ordered the hunter. "Make those posts firm again!" The men paid no attention.

Then the hunter hit the men with his bow to make them obey. The men struggled with the hunter, but they were no match for him. The strong hunter was able to control all three of them.

Eventually, the men did as the hunter said. They stopped digging and shoveled the dirt back in beside the posts. At last, all the posts were solidly set again.

After the posts were firm once more, the hunter returned home. The three thieves were sent to another part of the underworld to live.

The god told the people on earth what the hunter had done. The people thanked the hunter and then gave him many gifts—cloth, money, corn, and salt.

Thanks to the hunter, the earth was

saved from falling over. The gods then made sure that the earth was set so firmly that it could never fall. Now no one can dig up the posts anymore.

1. *How were the thieves causing trouble in the underworld?*
2. *Why was the hunter a good person to go to the underworld?*
3. *How was the hunter rewarded?*

The Deadly Game

This story comes from the Maya of Guatemala. Like the last story, it tells about a trip to the underworld. However, this story centers around a ball game called tlachtli. In ancient times, this game was popular among the Mayas.

The Underworld Rulers Trick the Twins

Long ago, there were twin brothers who were great tlachtli players. The brothers, named Hunhun-Ahpu and Vukub-Ahpu, played tlachtli all the time and won many games. They bragged that they were the best tlachtli players of all.

The rulers of the underworld heard the brothers bragging about their skill at tlachtli. The underworld rulers, named Hun-Camé and Vukub-Camé, also liked to play tlachtli. So they asked the brothers to come to the underworld to play a game and see who would win.

The twin brothers agreed to the game and traveled to the underworld. When they arrived, they were brought to a large room. The rulers of the underworld were sitting on thrones in the room. However, there were also several thrones with wooden statues. The statues looked so real that, by mistake, the twins bowed and spoke to one of the statues.

At this, Hun-Camé and Vukub-Camé started laughing. Then the twins realized that they had been tricked.

"How dare you mock us!" said Hunhun-Ahpu to the rulers of the underworld. "Stand up and fight us! Then we'll see who laughs!"

"All right," said Hun-Camé, "but first follow us."

The underworld rulers led the twins to another room and told them to sit down on two carved stones. When the twins sat down, they found out the stones were fiery hot. They jumped up, screaming with pain. Again, the underworld rulers laughed at the twins.

Next, the underworld rulers took the twins to a large, dark cave called the House of Gloom. The rulers gave each twin a torch made from reeds.

"These torches must be burning in the morning, or you shall die," Hun-Camé said to the twins.

Then the rulers left the twins in the cave.

Within a short time, the torches burned out. The twins waited in the dark cave until morning.

After the sun rose, the underworld rulers came back to the cave and saw that the torches had burned out. Then they carried out the threat and had the twins killed. The rulers buried the two bodies, except for the head of Hunhun-Ahpu. They hung his head in a tree, which immediately grew a large amount of fruit. The underworld rulers gave the order that no one could touch the tree or its fruit.

The Forbidden Fruit

One day, a young girl who lived in the underworld climbed into the fruit tree. She reached up to pick a piece of fruit. As she reached, the head of Hunhun-Ahpu spat into her hand.

"Go to earth right away!" said the head of Hunhun-Ahpu. "Your hand now holds my sons-to-be."

The girl was afraid and ran away from the underworld as fast as she could. She got to earth safely and went to live with the mother of the dead twins. In time, the girl gave birth to another set of twin boys. She named them Hunahpu and Xbalanque.

The boys grew up and became strong and smart. As young men, they started to play tlachtli as their father had. Soon they became skilled players.

The Twins Trick the Rulers of the Underworld

The rulers of the underworld heard of the twins practicing tlachtli. "Come down here and see if you can beat us," the underworld rulers challenged the twins.

So the young men went down to the underworld, taking along a pet bird. First, like their father, they were brought into the room with the wooden statues. The twins told their bird to peck the legs of everyone in the room. When the bird pecked the statues, nothing happened. When it pecked the real rulers of the underworld, however, the rulers screamed. In this way, Hunahpu and Xbalanque picked out the rulers from the statues.

Next, the young men were taken to the room with the hot stone chairs. They refused to sit on the chairs and sat on the floor instead.

Finally, the twins were led to the House of

Pecking the rulers' legs

Gloom. There, they were given torches.

Once again Hun-Camé said, "All these torches must be burning in the morning, or you shall die."

As soon as the underworld rulers left, the twins put out the torches. That way, the torches did not burn out. In the morning, the young men relit the torches.

When the underworld rulers saw the lit torches in the morning, they realized the young men had passed all their tests. Hun-Camé and Vukub-Camé had no choice but to play tlachtli with the twins.

Hunahpu and Xbalanque easily beat the underworld rulers in the tlachtli game. In anger, the rulers tried to kill the twins. They put the twins in the House of Cold. Then they put them in the House of Jaguars and then in the House of Fire. Then they put them in the House of Bats. In each house, the twins came up with a way to survive.

Finally, the twins realized their powers were as strong as those of the underworld rulers. The twins decided to use their powers against the rulers. The twins allowed Hun-Camé and Vukub-Camé to burn their bodies to ashes. The rulers then believed the twins were dead.

However, a few days later, the twins appeared in the underworld disguised as two old beggars. The beggars began performing magic tricks. They would burn houses, animals, and even themselves and then make everything reappear the same as before. Soon the beggars had attracted the attention of the rulers of the underworld.

Hun-Camé and Vukub-Camé asked the beggars to perform the burning magic on them. The beggars built a great fire and watched as the rulers of the underworld walked into it. However, this time, the beggars performed no magic. The underworld rulers did not reappear. The beggars then threw off their old clothes. They showed the people of the underworld that they were the twins.

"We came here to punish the rulers of the underworld for what they did to our father and his brother. Now they will never play tlachtli or rule over anyone again," said the twins.

After that, the twins rose into the sky and became the sun and the moon.

1. *Why did the first twins go to the underworld?*
2. *How did the pet bird help the second twins in the underworld?*
3. *What could the beggars do with their magic?*

The Land of the Dead

> This story about life after death comes from the
> Mískito of Nicaragua. In this myth, the land of
> the dead is called Mother Scorpion Country.

Naklili Goes with Kati

Once there was a man named Naklili,
who loved his wife, Kati, very much. One
day, however, Kati became sick and died.

Naklili could not bear to lose his wife, and
so he would not leave her grave. At the
grave, Kati's soul appeared to Naklili.

"I am going to Mother Scorpion now," Kati
told Naklili.

"Please, take me with you, Kati," said
Naklili.

"You know you cannot come with me,
Naklili. You are still alive. You must stay
with the living," answered Kati.

"I do not want to stay here without you. I
cannot be happy without you. Please, you
must take me with you," begged Naklili.

Kati finally gave in and said, "Take my
hand then and come with me."

The Journey

Kati led Naklili along a narrow trail that they had never traveled before. Along the trail, they came to a spot where the air was thick with flying moths. Kati did not want to go on, but Naklili scared the moths away from them. Then the two continued on their journey.

Next, they came to a place where two trees grew in the trail. The trees were very close together, and Kati could just pass between them. Naklili had to walk around the trees, though.

As Kati and Naklili walked on, the trail led to a gorge. Across the gorge was a threadlike bridge. A giant pot of boiling water was below the bridge. Because she was small and light, Kati could walk across the bridge. Naklili, however, knew the bridge was not wide or sturdy enough for him to cross. So Naklili jumped across the gorge.

Mother Scorpion Country

Naklili and Kati traveled together for a long time. Finally, they came to a wide river. On the other side of the river was Mother Scorpion Country. Naklili and Kati could see the happy souls there.

To cross the river, Naklili and Kati had to ride in a canoe paddled by a dog. In the river were sharks.

The dog said to Kati, "If a soul has lived a bad life, this canoe tips over and the sharks eat the soul. Those who have lived a good life cross the river safely."

Naklili and Kati reached the other side of the river safely. Many souls came to greet them, singing. Mother Scorpion, who was a tall woman, hugged Kati and welcomed her. Then the souls danced around Kati and took her to a great feast.

Mother Scorpion then looked angrily at Naklili. She said, "You do not belong here. Why did you come?"

"I love my wife very much. I cannot be happy without her. Please let me stay with her," said Naklili.

Then Mother Scorpion felt sorry for Naklili. "You may stay," she said. "but you are not like the others. You will not be happy here."

Kati was very happy in Mother Scorpion Country. No one had to work, and everyone had plenty to eat and drink. The trees were full of ripe fruit. The singing of birds filled the air.

Naklili could not be happy like Kati, however. Because he was different, he could not see the fruit trees or hear the birds singing. He missed his life on earth.

"Kati, I see that I do not belong here," Naklili said. "I want to go back to the land of the living."

"We will ask Mother Scorpion, and she will send you back," Kati said. "However, you must not tell anyone about the land of the dead until you are ready to return. When you want to come back, tell the story of where you have been. Then look above the door to our house. Take the beads that you find there."

So Mother Scorpion sent Naklili back to the land of the living. She put him inside a hollowed out bamboo tree. Then she set the tree in the river.

Naklili Returns to the Living

After a time, Naklili floated to the ocean. He finally drifted ashore, landing near his home. Naklili came out of the bamboo tree, and the first person he saw was his sister. She ran up to hug her brother.

"Oh, Naklili," said his sister, "I'm so happy to see you. Mother will be happy, too."

The brother and sister walked home together. As Naklili returned to his hut, his family and relatives came to greet him.

"Where have you been?" they asked.

Naklili remembered what his wife had told him and said nothing. However, the people did not understand why Naklili would not answer their questions. His relatives thought he acted strange, and so they stayed away from him. After a time, no one except his mother spoke to him.

Naklili grew lonely. He missed Kati. He found that he could not be happy in the land of the living either.

Naklili Goes Back to Mother Scorpion

One day, Naklili called the people of the village together. He told them about his trip to Mother Scorpion Country. He described the land of the dead.

Then Naklili went to the door of his hut. He reached up to grab the beads as Kati had told him to do.

The people screamed at Naklili, but it was too late. Instead of beads, Naklili grabbed a poisonous snake, which bit him. Naklili fell down and died. Soon he heard a voice.

"Naklili," Mother Scorpion called softly. "Welcome back."

1. *How were Naklili and Kati received in Mother Scorpion Country?*
2. *How did Kati feel in Mother Scorpion Country?*
3. *Why did Naklili want to return to the land of the living?*

The Ball of Thread

This Guatemalan story comes from the Maya. It is based on the idea that a huge horned snake lives under the ground. When the snake moves, the ground moves—and an earthquake results.

A material called maguey is important in this story. Maguey is a plant from which a hard fiber is obtained. The fiber is also called maguey.

Long ago in the land of the Maya, the earth rumbled and shook with great force. Houses fell down, and trees were uprooted.

The people hated the earthquakes and wanted them to stop. They talked among themselves about why the earth was shaking.

"The horned serpent who lives under the ground is moving and shaking the earth," they said. "Something must be bothering the snake. The old witch who lives in the cave is probably pestering the horned serpent. She is causing him pain, and so he writhes."

The people agreed that they should talk to their chief about the witch. So a small group went to speak with him.

"You must do something about the witch who lives in the cave," they said to the chief. "She is causing too much trouble. She won't leave the horned serpent alone, and he keeps shaking the earth. If you don't stop her, these earthquakes will never end."

The chief agreed to try to stop the witch. He told two men to go to the witch's cave and bring her back. The men followed the chief's orders and found the witch in her cave.

"Come with us," the men said to the witch. "The chief would like to speak with you now."

"All right," said the witch. "I will go to your chief. However, first let me say good-bye to my oarsmen."

On the floor of the cave, the witch had drawn a picture of a boat with two oarsmen. She walked over to the picture and jumped into it. The picture magically became a real boat in a stream of water. The two oarsmen rowed the witch away.

The chief's men could do nothing, so they went back to the chief. They told the chief how the witch had escaped through magic. The witch's trick greatly angered the chief.

"I hope she drowns in the water," said the chief.

For a time after that, the earthquakes stopped. Everyone's lives returned to normal. The chief and the people forgot about the witch. After a while, however, the trouble started again. The earth shook so violently that the rivers overflowed their banks and flooded the fields. The wild animals of the mountains sought refuge in the towns. Out of one mountain, the horned snake spat out fire and smoke and ashes.

Once again the people pleaded with their chief, "You must destroy this witch. Our cornfields are being ruined. You must burn the witch in the market square."

So the chief again ordered the same two men to go to the witch's cave and bring her back. Again, the men went to the witch's cave and found her there.

"You must come with us now," the two men told the witch. "Our chief wants to speak with you. You must not try to escape this time."

"Yes, I will go to see your chief now," the witch answered. "However, let me bring my ball of maguey thread."

So the witch picked up her ball of thread. Then she allowed the two men to lead her out of her cave and up to the market square.

At the square, a large crowd of people stood behind the chief. The people had come to see the witch thrown into a fire.

The men led the witch to the center of the square, where the chief stood.

The chief said to the witch, "The people say that you have been pestering the great horned snake. You are making him move and shake the earth. Our cornfields are being ruined. We cannot let you do this anymore."

The witch listened and then answered, "Yes, the horned snake has been moving a lot. I know the reason he writhes so much. He is restless because he has a worm in his tooth. The only cure is to give him a medicine from up in the clouds. I must go into the sky to get this medicine."

"If you can calm the horned snake, do it," the chief said.

The witch picked up a stick and shoved it into the ground. She tied one end of the maguey thread to the stick. Then she threw the ball of thread up into the air. As the thread unwound into the sky, the witch climbed up it. She quickly disappeared into the clouds.

The people never saw the witch again. In time, the earth calmed down.

1. *Why did the people want the chief to kill the witch?*
2. *How did the witch escape the first time?*
3. *How did the witch escape the second time?*

The First Monkeys

This story comes from the Maya of Guatemala. In it, five brothers are punished for being mean to their youngest brother.

A long time ago, there lived a woman with six sons. The five older sons hated the youngest son. They were always mean to their youngest brother.

One day, the five older sons had a dance at their house. They invited many people to the dance, but not their youngest brother.

During the dance, the youngest brother walked around outside the house. The older brothers would not let him inside. They made fun of him, calling him an orphan.

"The orphan can't dance," they said loudly so that everyone could hear. "He will never be able to dance as we do."

When it was time for everyone to eat, the table was filled with deer meat, chicken, and lamb. The older brothers still would not let the youngest brother come inside. After the older brothers finished eating, they threw their bones outside to him. "Here's some food for you, Orphan," they said, laughing.

A few days later, the youngest brother decided to have a dance of his own. He invited many people, including his brothers. On the day of the dance, he wore the finest clothes anyone had ever seen.

"Where did that boy get those clothes?" the older brothers asked their mother. "He has better clothes than anyone else."

"I don't know," answered the mother.

The next day, the older brothers were friendly to their youngest brother for the first time.

"We really liked the clothes you wore last night," they said. "It would be great if we could have fine clothes like that!"

"Well, come with me," said the youngest boy. "I'll show you where you can get such clothes."

The older brothers were thrilled. They walked happily through the forest with their youngest brother. They put their arms around his shoulder and patted him on the back.

The boy led his brothers to a wide, deep lake. He stopped by the lake.

"There, at the bottom of this lake, is where I got my clothes," the boy said. "All you have to do is drink up all of this water.

The youngest brother in his fine clothes

There are five of you, so you should be able to do it. Just drink up the water, and you'll find beautiful clothes like mine."

So the five brothers lay down along the shore of the lake. They started to drink the water. They drank for as long as they could. Finally, one of the brothers stood up.

"It's no use," said the brother. "There's no way we can drink up all of this water. It's impossible!"

"Well," said the young boy, "maybe you can get the clothes another way."

The boy pointed to a tall tree along the shore of the lake. At the top of the tree were fine clothes like the ones the boy had worn the night before.

"Look up there," said the boy, pointing to the top of the tree. "See the fine clothes! They're yours! All you have to do is climb the tree and get them."

The five brothers scrambled up the tree. Magically, the tree grew higher and higher. The brothers kept climbing, but they couldn't get to the clothes. Soon the five brothers were far up in the sky. Then the youngest brother laughed at them.

"You fools! You treated me like dirt. Now you will pay! From now on, you will eat the fruit that grows on trees and vines. You will make your home in the trees," the boy yelled.

Just then, the five brothers turned into monkeys. They stayed up in the tree and watched as the young boy walked back home alone.

In this way, the five mean brothers became the first monkeys.

1. *How did the five older brothers usually treat the youngest brother?*
2. *Why did the five older brothers start acting friendly toward the youngest brother?*
3. *Why did the five older brothers climb the tree?*

The First Grasshoppers

The Pipil of El Salvador tell this story about how the first grasshoppers appeared. In it, a greedy man is punished for mistreating his mother.

A long time ago, a woman had an only child, a son. The woman dearly loved her son. She took good care of him as he grew up.

When the woman's son became a man, he married and moved away. He started a farm and began planting corn. Before long, the man was growing a large amount of corn. In time, he grew rich selling corn.

Every week, the man's mother came to his house to get corn. One day, however, the man decided he would no longer share his corn with his mother. He forgot how well his mother had treated him. He had become greedy and thoughtless.

The man told his wife, "If my mother comes here again, don't give her any corn. If she comes while I'm eating, put the food away. I won't have her eating with me. I don't want that old woman coming here anymore."

Near lunch time the next day, the man's

mother came walking toward the house. The man was just about to eat. When his wife saw the old woman, she quickly put the food away. Then the wife went outside and called the dogs.

"Go get her," the wife yelled to the dogs.

The dogs ran out and bit the old woman. Without a word, the woman turned and went back home.

Then the wife set the food out on the table again for her husband to eat. After he finished eating, the man lay down to take a nap and fell asleep.

Suddenly, the man awoke. He heard a noise in the cupboard where the corn was kept. The man went to the cupboard and opened the door. As soon as the door opened, grasshoppers jumped out on the man. They covered the man and ate him. Then they attacked the man's wife and children and ate them too.

The grasshoppers flew out of the man's house. They increased in number and spread out all over the world.

Soon the people who lived near the man found out what had happened. They said, "The grasshoppers killed the man and his family because he was greedy. He did not

The grasshoppers in the cupboard

share even with his own mother."

Now, when grasshoppers come, they strip some cornfields bare but not others. They attack the fields of people who are like the greedy man.

1. *How did the man become rich?*
2. *What orders did the man give his wife?*
3. *Why did the grasshoppers eat the man and his family?*

The Foolish Jaguar

This story comes from Panama. It tells about a rabbit who plays a trick on a jaguar, a large, wild cat of Central and South America. Stories in which animals play tricks on one another or on people are called trickster tales. This kind of story is common in many parts of the world, including Central America. In these tales, animals can talk to each other and to people.

Other versions of this story are told in other cultures.

Once there was a man who made his living selling cheese. At an outside market, he sold balls of cheese wrapped in green banana leaves.

One night, the man was walking home with the balls of cheese he had not sold that day. A rabbit decided to do the man a favor.

Walking up to the man, Rabbit said, "I see that your banana leaves are all dried out. I've brought you some new, green leaves. They will help keep your cheese fresh."

"Thank you," said the man. "Let me repay you with these two balls of cheese."

Rabbit took the two balls of cheese from the man and put them in his pocket. Then he went on his way home. The path to Rabbit's home wound along a river.

As he walked along the river, Rabbit thought, "Oh, the moon is so full and bright. What a good night for fishing! When I get home, I'll get my pole and see if I can catch some fish."

So when Rabbit got home, he took his fishing pole and went back to the river. It was indeed a good night for fishing, and he began catching fish right away. He was so busy fishing that he did not notice a jaguar creeping up behind him.

Jaguar grabbed Rabbit and said, "I've caught you! What a tasty meal you'll make."

Rabbit acted calmly. He answered, "Take it easy, Jaguar."

Then Rabbit took a ball of cheese out of his pocket and bit into it.

"This is the best cheese I've ever had," said Rabbit. "Would you like some?"

Rabbit took out the other ball of cheese and handed it to Jaguar.

Jaguar bit into the cheese ball and said, "I love this cheese. Where did you get it?"

"Oh, there's lots of this cheese at the

bottom of the river. Just look! See that big cheese ball down in the river?" Rabbit said. He pointed to the moon's reflection in the river.

"Oh, yes," Jaguar said, excitedly. "It looks like it's near the top of the river, though."

"It looks that way, but it isn't," Rabbit said. "It's just that the water is so clear. The cheese is really on the bottom of the river."

Jaguar thought for a minute. Then he looked all around the riverbank, which had many big rocks. Finally, he spoke.

"Rabbit, I know I can't dive to the bottom of the river. It's too deep. Will you tie two of these big rocks to my feet? Then I can sink to the bottom and get the cheese," Jaguar said.

"That's a great idea!" Rabbit answered.

Rabbit quickly tore some vines from a tree on the riverbank. Using the vines, he tied the rocks onto Jaguar's feet. Then he pushed Jaguar into the river. Jaguar sank to the bottom of the river. As he hit the river bottom, he saw that there was no cheese. He realized that Rabbit had tricked him.

Jaguar untied all the vines as fast as he could. Then he swam back up to the river's surface. By the time Jaguar reached the top, however, Rabbit was safe at home.

1. *Where did Rabbit get the two balls of cheese?*
2. *How did Rabbit convince Jaguar to go into the river?*
3. *What did Jaguar realize when he reached the bottom of the river?*

The Buzzard's Bald Head

This animal tale comes from Nicaragua. Like the last story, this one features Rabbit. In the story, a buzzard tries to get even with Rabbit, who has played many tricks on him.

This tale explains how buzzards came to have bald heads.

Rabbit used to play many tricks on Buzzard. This made Buzzard angry, and he planned a way to get even with Rabbit.

One day, Rabbit was picking berries from a bush and eating them. Buzzard flew up to Rabbit and acted happy to see him.

"Hello, Rabbit. How are you doing?"

"Hello. I'm fine, thank you," said Rabbit. "I'm eating these delicious berries. Would you like some?"

"No, thanks," Buzzard said. "If you like berries, you should come to one of our feasts up in the clouds. At these feasts, we birds have the best fruits imaginable! I'll make a deal with you. If you'll bring your guitar and play some music, I'll take you to a feast in the clouds right now."

"That sounds wonderful! Wait just a minute, and I'll hurry and get my guitar," Rabbit answered.

Rabbit ran back home and got his guitar. Within a short time, he returned to the berry bush where Buzzard was waiting.

"Now hop on my back, and we'll be off," said Buzzard.

Rabbit jumped on Buzzard's back. Then Buzzard took off and flew high into the sky. Soon the two of them were nearing the clouds.

"All right now, Rabbit," said Buzzard suddenly. "You've played a lot of tricks on me. Let's see how you like this trick!"

Then Buzzard started to fly crazily. He flew in circles, upside down, straight up, and straight down. He tried everything to make Rabbit fall off.

Rabbit did not fall off, however. He held on as tightly as he could.

"Stop this crazy flying!" yelled Rabbit.

Of course, Buzzard would not stop. He kept trying to make Rabbit fall.

Finally, Rabbit hit Buzzard hard over the head with his guitar. Buzzard's head got stuck in the guitar. Buzzard was stunned and started to fall rapidly to the ground.

Acting quickly, Rabbit held out Buzzard's wings so that the two animals floated safely to the ground. Once on the ground, Rabbit jumped off Buzzard's back.

Awakening, Buzzard yelled, "Get this guitar off of my head, Rabbit!"

"Get it off yourself, Buzzard. Maybe now you'll think twice before you play another trick on me."

Buzzard pulled on the guitar, but it wouldn't come off easily. He kept pulling and pulling until he finally got the guitar off. However, the feathers on the bird's head came off with the guitar.

Ever since then, buzzards have had bald heads.

1. *Why did Buzzard want to play a trick on Rabbit?*
2. *How did Buzzard convince Rabbit to ride on his back?*
3. *How did Buzzard tear the feathers off his head?*

The Leaf Animal

In another tale from Nicaragua, the people of a village want to get rid of Rabbit. They do not succeed, however, and once again Rabbit plays the last trick.

For many years, Rabbit played tricks on the people in a village in Nicaragua. The people grew tired of Rabbit's tricks, and they complained to their king.

The king said, "Yes, I know that Rabbit does nothing but cause trouble. Why don't you go out and catch him? Then bring him to me, and I will do away with him."

So the people left the palace and talked among themselves. They discussed a number of ways to catch Rabbit.

Finally, one person said, "I have an idea! We all know that all the animals come to the water hole to drink. Rabbit drinks at the water hole when he gets thirsty, too. If we hide there, we can catch him!"

The people all agreed that this was a good plan. However, they did not realize that Rabbit was hiding behind a bush, listening.

"We'll see if these people can catch me!"

said Rabbit, giving a big laugh.

Then Rabbit went on his way. He walked to another village. Going through the village, he came to a shoe store. The shoemaker was sitting outside the store, next to a pair of shoes he had made.

"Hello, sir. My, this is a hot day, isn't it?" said Rabbit in a friendly voice.

"Oh, yes, it is. This is one of the hottest days we have had in a long time," the shoemaker answered.

"If I were you, I'd go inside to cool off. I imagine that you'd enjoy some cold water to drink," Rabbit said.

"You know, I think you're right," said the shoemaker. "That's just what I need."

So the shoemaker went inside. As soon as the shoemaker was out of sight, Rabbit took the pair of shoes. Off he hopped, out of the village and down the road.

Along the road, Rabbit spotted a man in the distance walking toward him. The man was carrying a large gourd.

"I bet that man is carrying honey," Rabbit thought. "I do believe I would like to have some honey."

So Rabbit thought of a plan to get the gourd. He dropped one of the shoes in the road. Then he hopped behind some bushes to hide there.

After a time, the man came along and saw the shoe in the road. He picked up the shoe and then looked around for the other one. Of course, he couldn't find the other shoe anywhere.

"What can I do with just one shoe?" thought the man. So he dropped the shoe and walked on.

This was just what Rabbit had hoped would happen. Rabbit ran ahead, staying out of sight behind the bushes along the side of the road. He got ahead of the man and tossed the other shoe in the road. Then he waited in the bushes for the man to come along.

Within a short time, the man came to the shoe that Rabbit had tossed in the road.

Picking up the shoe, the man thought, "This shoe matches the other one. I'll just put down this heavy gourd and quickly go back and get the other shoe."

So the man put down the gourd and ran back to get the other shoe. In an instant, Rabbit hopped out, grabbed the gourd, and scurried away into the forest.

Soon Rabbit came to an open spot in the forest, covered with fallen leaves. Rabbit stopped and opened the gourd. It was indeed filled with honey as he had suspected.

Rabbit ate honey until he was full. Then he poured the rest of the honey over his body. He made sure every inch of his body was covered.

Sticky with honey, Rabbit rolled over in the leaves. He kept rolling until leaves stuck to his whole body. Rabbit looked like the strangest animal imaginable. He was a great mass of walking leaves!

Off Rabbit hopped to the village. As he passed down the street, all the people looked in wonder. "What kind of animal is this?" they thought.

Rabbit hopped straight to the water hole. The people were all hiding in the bushes, waiting. They did not recognize Rabbit, however. Rabbit went right up to the water and took a big drink. He drank all the water he wanted.

Then Rabbit hopped away safely.

1. *How did the people plan to catch Rabbit?*
2. *What trick did Rabbit play to get the man's honey?*
3. *How was Rabbit able to get a drink of water without being recognized?*

The Frog's Crooked Legs

This story from the Maya of Guatemala explains why the frog has bent legs. The Maya say that long ago, the frog used to walk on two legs as people do. The frog's arms and legs became bent after a terrible fall.

One day, the birds in the jungle were making plans to fly to heaven and sing a concert for God. One of the birds was Crow.

Now Crow was a friend of Frog's, and she told Frog about the birds' plans.

"Oh, please take me along with you," Frog begged Crow. "I would love to see what heaven is like."

"No, I can't do that," said Crow. "You're not a bird, and only birds are going."

Frog begged and begged, but Crow kept saying no. Finally, Frog decided to get to heaven by trickery.

"Okay, Crow, I give up," Frog said. "I know I can't go to heaven, but will you give God a gift from me?"

"Yes, I'd be happy to do that," answered Crow. "I'll pick the gift up tomorrow morning before I leave."

"Thanks so much," said Frog. "I'll put it on my doorstep for you."

The next morning Crow picked up the package that was sitting on Frog's doorstep. Then she joined the other birds and flew off to heaven.

When the birds arrived in heaven, they went straight to God's throne room. Before entering the room, Crow put down Frog's package near the door.

Once inside the throne room, the birds began their concert before God. Their singing was beautiful, and God was enjoying the concert.

Suddenly there was a loud croaking from the back of the room. Everyone turned to look, and there was Frog.

"What are you doing here? How did you get here?" asked Crow.

"I came in the package you carried. I just hopped out," said Frog, laughing.

"Well, you won't go back that way!" said Crow angrily.

The birds then continued their singing. After the concert was over, all the birds flew back to earth. Since Crow would not take her along, Frog remained in heaven. She thought and thought about how to get back

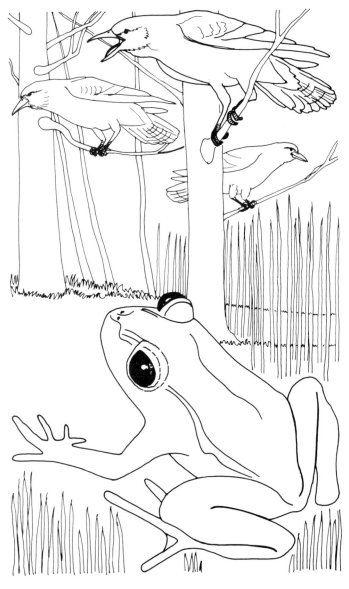

Frog's fall

to earth. Finally, Frog decided she would risk jumping.

So Frog took a great leap and fell down to earth. It was a long fall, but luckily, she only broke her arms and legs. She was never the same again, however. From that time on, her arms and legs were crooked. When she hopped, her belly was close to the ground.

Since that time, frogs have hopped on four bent legs.

1. *Why were the birds going to heaven?*
2. *How did Frog get to heaven?*
3. *How did Frog get back to earth?*

The Woodpecker's Warning

This story comes from the Maya of Guatemala. The tale centers around a Maya belief about woodpeckers. The Maya thought that woodpeckers warned people of trouble.

Once there was a man who lived on a large farm called a *hacienda*. The hacienda was far from any town. The nearest town was Cobán, which took four days to reach. Once a month, the man would go to Cobán to buy supplies for his hacienda.

One day, the man and one of his servants were returning from Cobán. The man was riding a horse. The servant was leading another horse loaded with the supplies the man had just bought. The road led up a mountain.

As the man and his servant were going up the mountain, they decided to rest under a tree. The man got off his horse and went to sit down in the shade. His servant followed him and sat down also.

Suddenly, a woodpecker began singing in the tree.

The servant said to the man, "Did you

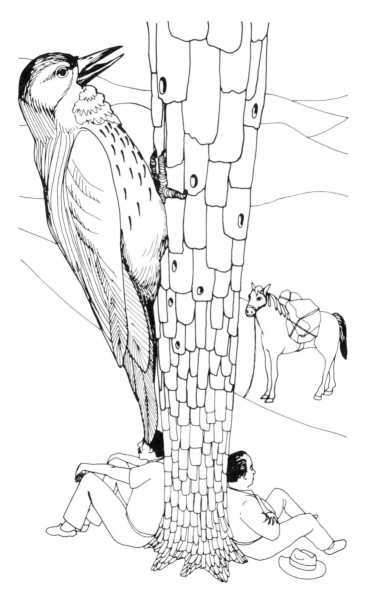

The woodpecker singing

hear the woodpecker singing? That means something bad will happen to us on this road. We cannot go on."

"Don't be silly," said the man. "We have to go on. We must return home. That's just a foolish idea of yours. The woodpecker's singing means nothing."

"No! No! I cannot go on," the servant insisted. "Something bad will happen. I know it! The woodpecker always warns us of danger ahead."

The man stood up, mounted his horse, and started on the road. "Come on," he called to the servant. "We are going on."

The servant would not get up, however. He stayed under the tree and would not move. The man became angry because his servant would not obey him. He got off his horse and strode over to the servant. The man started to beat the servant.

"You do what I tell you to do," the man yelled at the servant.

After the man stopped hitting him, the servant said, "All right. Now I will go with you. The bad thing has already happened. The woodpecker was warning me that you would beat me, and you did. Now I can go on with you because I don't have to worry about something bad happening anymore."

So the two men continued down the road and returned to the hacienda.

1. *What happened when the man and the servant stopped to rest?*
2. *What did the servant believe the woodpecker's singing meant?*
3. *Why did the servant finally agree to continue on the trip home?*

Pronunciation Guide

> Every effort has been made to present native pronunciations of the unusual names in this book. Sometimes experts differed in their opinions, however, or no pronunciation could be found. Also, certain foreign-language sounds were felt to be unpronounceable by today's readers. In these cases, editorial license was exercised in selecting pronunciations.

Key

The letter or letters used to show pronunciation have the following sounds:

a	as in *map* and *glad*
ah	as in *pot* and *cart*
aw	as in *fall* and *lost*
ch	as in *chair* and *child*
e	as in *let* and *care*
ee	as in *feet* and *please*
ey	as in *play* and *face*
g	as in *gold* and *girl*
hy	as in *huge* and *humor*
i	as in *my* and *high*
ih	as in *sit* and *clear*

j	as in *jelly* and *gentle*
k	as in *skill* and *can*
ky	as in *cute*
l	as in *long* and *pull*
my	as in *mule*
ng	as in *sing* and *long*
ny	as in *canyon* and *onion*
o	as in *slow* and *go*
oo	as in *cool* and *move*
ow	as in *cow* and *round*
s	as in *soon* and *cent*
sh	as in *shoe* and *sugar*
th	as in *thin* and *myth*
u	as in *put* and *look*
uh	as in *run* and *up*
y	as in *you* and *yesterday*
z	as in *zoo* and *pairs*

Guide

Capital letters are used to represent stressed syllables. For example, the word *ugly* would be written here as "UHG lee."

Cabécar: kah BEY kahr

Cakchiquel: kahk chee KEYL

chirimía: chee ree MEE ah

Chorti: chor TEE

Cuna: KOO nah

hacienda: ah see EN dah

Hunahpu: oo NAH poo

Hun-Camé: oon kah MEY

Hunhun-Ahpu: oon oon AH poo

Ixil: EE seel

Jicaque: hee KAH key

Kanhobal: kahn O bahl

Kekchi: keyk CHEE

maguey: mah GEY

Mam: MAHM

Maya: MI ah

Mískito: MEES kee to

Mopan: MO pahn

Naklili: nahk LEE lee

Nima-cux: nee mah KOOKS

Olocupinele: o lo koo pee NEY ley

Piler: pee LEYR

Pipil: pee PEEL

Popol Vuh: PO pul VOO

Quiche: kee CHEY

Sibú: see BOO

Sipac: see PAHK

tlachtli: TLAHCH tlee

Tzutuhil: tsoo TOO heel

Vukub-Ahpu: voo koob AH poo

Vukub-Camé: voo koob kah MEY

Xbalanque: sbah LAHN key